Where Is Daddy?
Who Is Daddy?

by Azaliya Schulz, Nastasia Yakovleva

Illustrated by Daria Volkova

Where is Daddy? Who is Daddy?

Azaliya Schulz and Nastasia Yakovleva.
Illustrated by Daria Volkova,

For permission requests, e-mail llcthingsthatmatter@gmail.com

ISBN: 978-1-7378727-0-2 (printed paperback edition)
ISBN: 978-1-7378727-1-9 (e-book)

Library of Congress Control Number: 2021920287

Printed in The Unites States of America.

First printing 2021.

This book belongs to

The day you were born was **the best day** in the lives of your mommy and daddy. When they saw you for the first time, they instantly fell in love with you.

They held you and hugged you; they nuzzled you and cuddled you. They rocked you and fed you and **loved you**.

Your mommy and daddy prayed to God to give you the best qualities each of them had.

Your mommy wanted to give you her **kindness**,

her **resourcefulness,**

her **resilience,**

and her **wisdom.**

Your daddy wanted to give you his **curiosity**,

his **courage**,

his **strength,**

and his **humility.**

God smiled down on them, and their wishes came true.

You were the **kindest,**

the **strongest,**

the **wisest,**

and the most **curious.**

You were **humble,**

and **resourceful,**

courageous

and **resilient.**

When your mommy and daddy looked at you, they were so happy! You were **the best child they could have ever wished for**. They were grateful to each other and the whole universe for you!

Each of them had their path to follow, and the time came for them to say goodbye. Your mommy and daddy thanked and hugged each other, and they hugged you, knowing that they will forever be your parents and that you were **the best gift** they were ever given.

But you may still wonder ...

"Who is my daddy,
          and where is he now?"

I will tell you, my child.

Your daddy is right here. He is inside of you. He is the bravest, the strongest, and the most curious part of you.

Your daddy lives in your soul.
Your daddy lives in your heart.

That is where your daddy is, my child.

And wherever you go, **he lives forever in you**.

Your notes

2021

Made in the USA
Las Vegas, NV
27 December 2023